W9-CZW-754

Film It!

YouTube Projects for the Real World

Carolyn Bernhardt

Checkerboard Library

An Imprint of Abdo Publishing
abdopublishing.com

abdopublishing.com

Published by Abdo Publishing, a division of ABDO, PO Box 398166, Minneapolis, Minnesota 55439. Copyright © 2017 by Abdo Consulting Group, Inc. International copyrights reserved in all countries. No part of this book may be reproduced in any form without written permission from the publisher. Checkerboard Library™ is a trademark and logo of Abdo Publishing.

Printed in the United States of America, North Mankato, Minnesota

062016
092016

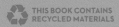
THIS BOOK CONTAINS RECYCLED MATERIALS

Content Developer: Nancy Tuminelly
Design and Production: Mighty Media, Inc.
Series Editor: Liz Salzmann
Photo Credits: Alamy; iStockphoto; Mighty Media, Inc.; Shutterstock

The following manufacturers/names appearing in this book are trademarks: Dixon®, Elmer's®, Office Depot®, Sharpie®

Publishers Cataloging-in-Publication Data
Names: Bernhardt, Carolyn, author.
Title: Film it! : YouTube projects for the real world / by Carolyn Bernhardt.
Description: Minneapolis, MN : Abdo Publishing, [2017] | Series: Cool social media | Includes bibliographical references and index.
Identifiers: LCCN 2016936497 | ISBN 9781680783568 (lib. bdg.) | ISBN 9781680790245 (ebook)
Subjects: LCSH: YouTube (Firm)--Juvenile literature. | YouTube (Electronic resource)--Juvenile literature. | Online social networks--Juvenile literature. | Internet industry--Juvenile literature. | Internet security measures--Juvenile literature.
Classification: DDC 006.7--dc23
LC record available at /http://lccn.loc.gov/2016936497

Contents

What Is YouTube?

You create a cool dance to a popular new hip-hop song. Your friend films you dancing to the music in a park. The video turns out really well! You decide to **upload** it **online** as a tutorial. Your dad helps you post the video on YouTube. When you and your dad log in to the account the next day, you see that the video has been viewed thousands of times! You're a social media star! This is the fun of YouTube.

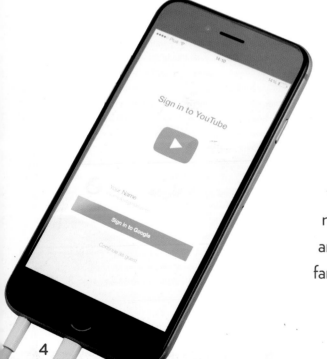

YouTube is a video-sharing website and app. YouTubers create and post videos on all sorts of topics, including music videos, tutorials, silly animal videos, and more. Some users have even become famous from their YouTube videos!

Interaction is a major part of YouTube. Users like, comment on, and learn from one another's videos. This creates **online** communities. YouTubers from all over the world share creative ideas and inspire one another to create interesting content.

YouTube
Site Bytes

Purpose: sharing videos

Type of Service: website and app
URL: www.youtube.com
App name: YouTube

Date of Founding: February 2005

Founders: Steve Chen, Chad Hurley, and Jawed Karim

Compatible Devices:

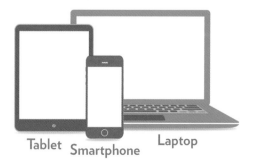

Tablet Smartphone Laptop

Tech Terms:

Streaming

Streaming is watching video content live. YouTubers get **permission** from YouTube to **upload** live videos. This allows them to send content to YouTube as they are shooting it. The content instantly becomes visible to viewers.

Channel

A YouTube channel is a collection of videos from the same user. Users can subscribe to YouTube channels to receive alerts when new content is uploaded.

Founding **YouTube**

Steve Chen, Chad Hurley, and Jawed Karim met while working at PayPal, an e-payment website. They discussed many Internet start-up ideas before creating YouTube. The founders launched YouTube in May 2005. It was meant to be a video dating service. But users **uploaded** videos of all kinds. Soon, these videos were getting millions of views a day!

Technology company Google purchased YouTube from Chen, Hurley, and Karim in November 2006. Since then, YouTube has continued to grow in popularity.

Steve Chen

Chad Hurley

Jawed Karim

Account Info:

- Users must be at least 13 to create an account.

- Users can create accounts on YouTube's website. They can also **download** the YouTube app to smartphones or tablets.

- Only people with YouTube accounts may upload videos.

- Anyone can view YouTube videos posted to public accounts. Videos posted to private accounts can only be viewed by people chosen by the original poster.

- People with YouTube accounts can like and comment on videos.

Supplies

Here are some of the materials, tools, and devices you'll need to do the projects in this book.

markers

corkboard

index cards

clear tape

craft glue

scissors

printer (loaded with paper and ink)

notebook

pushpins

stapler

tablet

smartphone

Staying Safe

The Internet is a great resource for information. And using it can be a lot of fun! But staying safe **online** is most important. Follow these tips to use social media safely.

* Never try to sign up for a social media account if you are underage. YouTube users must be at least 13 years old.

* Don't share personal information online, especially information people can use to find you in real life. This includes your telephone number and home address.

* Be kind online! Remember that real people post content on the Internet. Do not post rude, hurtful, or mean comments. Report any instances of **cyberbullying** you see to a trusted adult.

* In addition to cyberbullying, report any **inappropriate** content to a trusted adult.

Safety Symbol

Some projects in this book require searching on the Internet. That means these projects need some adult help. Determine if you'll need help on a project by looking for this safety symbol.

Internet Use
This project requires searching on the Internet.

9

Graphic Match Flip-Book

Learn about film transitions by making a fun flip-book!

What you need

- » computer, tablet, or smartphone
- » notebook
- » pencil
- » printer
- » scissors
- » optional: paper, colored pencils, markers
- » stapler

Successful YouTubers work to improve their filmmaking skills in order to make the best videos. One important part of filmmaking is **graphic** match. This is showing similar-looking backgrounds, people, or props from one scene to the next. It helps a video smoothly **transition** between scenes. For example, a scene in an empty parking lot transitions nicely into a scene in the desert because both places are large, flat, and bare. In contrast, transitioning quickly from a desert to a mountain scene can be jarring for the viewer. Create a fun flip-book to learn how to spot and create graphic matches.

1. Have an adult help you find videos about graphic matching on YouTube. Watch the videos to learn more about graphic matching. Take notes to help you remember what you learn.

2. Have an adult help you find images of scenery **online**. These could include mountains, forests, fields, or oceans. Print ten different images.

3. Trim the photos to be the same size.

(continued on the next page)

4. Find **graphic** matches in your photos. Start by grouping the ones that are the most similar together.

5. Then look for which photos seem to make the best **transitions** between groups. Line the photos up with these transition photos connecting the groups.

6. If you are struggling to find transitions for your photos, create your own! Cut a sheet of paper to the size of your images. Draw a picture that will help create a graphic match.

7. Pile the photos in the order you lined them up. Staple them together along the left edge.

8. Flip through the photos and watch them transition beautifully!

#funfact
The very first YouTube video was of one of the founders looking at elephants at the San Diego Zoo in California.

Podcast Lab

Practice making podcasts to learn how podcast stars keep listeners entertained!

What you need
» notebook
» pen
» index cards
» voice recorder

Many YouTube stars make podcasts, which are recordings that can be **downloaded** and watched later. Today, podcasts include video, but they were originally sound recordings only. What makes these recordings exciting to listen to? How hard is it to create interesting content without video? Find out by creating your own podcast and sharing it with friends and family members. Will your podcast keep them entertained?

1. Think of a topic you know a lot about. This could be your favorite sport, food, movie, or somewhere you have traveled.

2. Write down what interesting things you could say about your topic. What makes the topic you chose your favorite? What do most people like about it? What are some super-cool facts about your topic? Do you know any funny stories related to your topic? What else about it might be fun for listeners to hear?

3. Write your main points on index cards. This will help you remember what you want to say. But don't write a complete **script**. Podcasts are more like a discussion than a report.

4. Record yourself talking about your topic. Avoid pausing for too long or saying "um" or "uh" too much. You want to keep your listeners interested. Make as many recordings as it takes to create a podcast you are happy with. This could take a long time, but that's okay!

5. Have your friends and family members listen to your podcast. Did it interest them all the way to the end? Could they hear and understand everything you said? Would they listen to another podcast made by you? Think about what went well and what you would change for your next podcast. Then start recording!

#funfact
The Apple store iTunes has a special page that offers podcasts hosted by YouTubers and other web video personalities.

4

5

15

YouTube Teacher

Record a tutorial to teach your friends and family members something new!

What you need

- » notebook
- » pencil
- » supplies & props for the tutorial
- » video camera, tablet, or smartphone
- » optional: computer & video-editing software

YouTubers **upload** tutorial videos about many different topics. Tutorials show how to do things such as play an instrument or bake a cake. It is easier to learn by seeing than reading steps. Teach your friends and family members a new skill in a video tutorial inspired by YouTube!

1. Think about a skill you have. This could be anything! Maybe you are great at a snowboarding move or making paper crafts. Or maybe you have a trick to memorizing the capitals of all 50 states.

2. Write down your skill in a notebook. Think about how you would teach this skill to others. What key points would you make? How would you show the physical parts of your skill? What props would you need? Write down your ideas.

3. Turn your notes into a **script** for your video. Write what you will say and do in each scene.

(continued on the next page)

2

3

4. Gather any props or supplies you'll need for your tutorial. Then, find somewhere to record it.

5. Think about how best to frame your tutorial. This might mean shooting full-body shots to show a dance move, or close-ups of your hands to teach paper folding. Set up your camera however will best capture what you want to show. Or, have a friend or family member help record your tutorial.

6. Begin your video by introducing yourself and your topic.

7. Tell your viewers what supplies they need to successfully complete your lesson. Show the supplies you've gathered as examples.

8. Film the key points from your **script**. Explain each action as you do it. Write tips or main points on a whiteboard, chalkboard, or piece of paper if you like. You can also include jokes or fun facts. Be creative! But be sure your tutorial stays focused on what you're teaching.

9. If you have a computer and the necessary **software**, edit your video. For example, you could add fun effects, background music, and more. But remember that the purpose of your tutorial is to teach. Be careful you don't add elements that distract from the video's content.

10. Create an **evaluation** form for viewers. This form should include questions like "Did the teacher make the information fun to learn?", "Was the information easy to understand?", and "What could the teacher have done differently to improve the lesson?"

11. Have your friends and family members watch your tutorial. Give them each an evaluation form to fill out. Observe them as they watch the video. Discuss their evaluations. Were you successful in teaching the skill? What would you do differently in your next YouTube-inspired tutorial?

Origami Box Tutorial Evaluation Name:_____

1. What was your favorite part of the tutorial?

2. Was the teacher good at explaining the activity?

3. Did you ____ the pace of the tutorial? Was it too slow, too fast, or just ____

____ that could the teacher do better?

What did the teacher do well?

10

____ivities would ____

11

19

Stop-Motion Shoot

Magically create action by moving
objects behind the scenes!

What you need

» objects to shoot
» video camera, tablet, or smartphone
» computer
» video-editing software

Stop-motion is a way of making a film or video. Filmmakers use it to create action with a series of still images or short videos. Filmmakers move the objects slightly between shots. When all the shots are put together, it looks like the objects are moving. Create your own stop-motion story with toys, clay, or even foods!

1. Find small objects you want to film. These could be action figures, toys, shells, or anything else you can think of!

2. Think about a short action scene for your objects. What story will the scene tell? What movements will your objects make?

3. Place the camera wherever you want it to shoot the action. Secure the camera so it is always in the same place as you film. Set up the first scene.

#funfact
At the end of 2015, more than 400 hours of video was **uploaded** to YouTube each minute.

(continued on the next page)

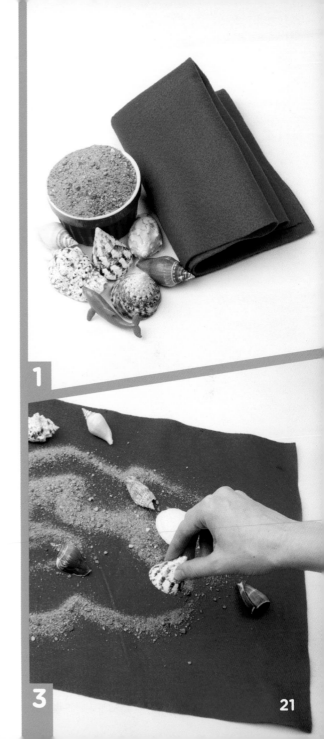

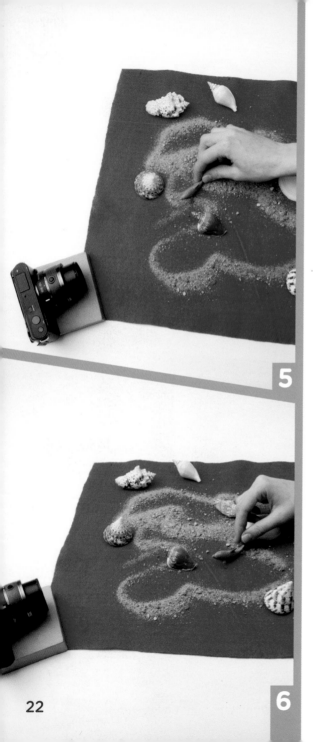

4. Record the scene for a few seconds.

5. Move one or more objects very slightly. For example, your video might be of a dolphin swimming. Move the dolphin forward a little bit. Record the scene for a few seconds.

6. Continue to move objects slightly, recording a few seconds each time.

7. **Upload** your video recordings to your computer. Use editing **software** to cut and arrange them.

8. String the recordings together into one video. If your editing software allows it, add fun sounds or other effects.

9. Show your video to your friends and family!

#funfact

On **mobile** devices, YouTube users spend about 40 minutes watching videos every time they open the app.

7

9

SkitTube

Perform skits selected by your audience!

SkitTube — Adventures in Space

Astronauts at Dinner!
What happens when four astronauts try to gather around the dinner table without any gravity?!

Elephants on the moon!
How would elephants explore the moon?

making friends on
who would we meet
we went to mars?

Galactic Olym
what would the olympic games
look like in outer space?

What you need
» notebook
» pencil
» computer, tablet, or smartphone
» poster board
» markers
» ruler
» scissors
» craft glue
» stage or performance space
» friends & family members

When a viewer searches a topic on YouTube, the site lists a number of videos on the topic. Then the viewer can choose which video to watch. Provide an **audience** with the same experience! Plan a series of **skits** where the audience members choose which one they'll see next!

1. Write four or five skits on the same topic. Possible topics might include the jungle, outer space, or school. The skits should be short and easy to act out.

2. Have an adult help you search for videos on YouTube. Look for videos on specific topics. Note what the search results look like. What kind of information is included in the results?

3. Make a poster that looks like YouTube search results. Write the topic of your skits at the top of the poster board.

(continued on the next page)

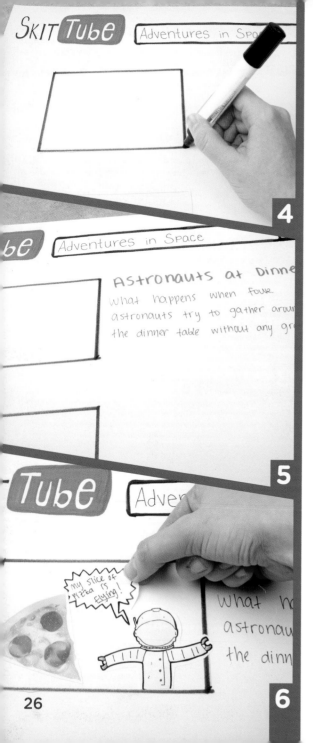

4. Use a ruler and pencil to draw a box for each **skit** under the topic. Trace over the pencil lines with marker.

5. Write information about the skits next to the boxes.

6. Draw or glue pictures that show what the skits are about inside the boxes. If you look for photos **online**, be sure to have an adult help out.

7. Set the poster next to your stage.

#funfact
When YouTube is **buffering**, users can press an arrow key to play a game called Snake.

8. Find some friends and family members who want to be in the **skits**. Practice each skit until all of the actors know their parts. Then, it's showtime!

9. Gather your **audience**. Show the audience members the poster. Ask them to vote for which skit they want to see first.

10. After you perform the skit, have the audience vote on which one to see next. Continue until the audience has seen all of the skits.

11. Think about your performances. In what order did the audience choose to see the skits? How did this affect the show? Did the order make the show funny, silly, or dramatic?

8

9

Storyboard

Sketch scenes to create
a video storyboard!

What you need

- » index cards
- » markers
- » corkboard
- » pushpins
- » camera, tablet, or smartphone
- » any props, costumes, or actors needed for the video

28

Many YouTube video creators plan what they are going to make before they record anything. A good way to plan a film is by storyboarding. This is drawing a sketch of each scene in a video. Create your own storyboard. Then, follow it as you film to see how well it tells the story!

1. Think of a story you want to tell in a video. What should the very first shot of your video look like? Draw this scene on an index card.

2. Draw the rest of the scenes on index cards.

3. Arrange the index cards on corkboard. Place them in the correct order to tell the story.

#funfact
YouTube has more than 1 billion users.

(continued on the next page)

4. Use pushpins to hold the index cards in place. Take a photo of this arrangement. Then you can refer to it easily later as you are recording.

5. Now you are ready to begin shooting your video! Gather any props you need. Ask friends and family to be actors if needed.

6. Film a scene for each image on your storyboard.

7. Watch your film. How did it turn out? Does the story make sense? Was your storyboard arrangement helpful? What would you do differently next time? Gather or draw images to add to your storyboard, or make another one. Keep planning, arranging, and having fun filming!

Glossary

audience – a group of people watching a performance.

buffer – to store or collect data while it is being transferred or processed.

cyberbully – to tease, hurt, or threaten someone online.

download – to transfer data from a computer network to a single computer or device.

evaluation – the process or instance of determining the meaning or worth of something.

graphic – of or relating to visual arts such as painting, film, and photography.

inappropriate – not suitable, fitting, or proper.

mobile – capable of moving or being moved.

online – connected to the Internet.

permission – formal consent.

script – the written text for a performance.

skit – a short, funny play or performance.

software – the written programs used to operate a computer.

technology – the science of how something works.

transition – to move from one style, stage, or form to another.

upload – to transfer data from a computer to a larger network.

Websites

To learn more about Cool Social Media, visit **booklinks.abdopublishing.com**. These links are routinely monitored and updated to provide the most current information available.

Index

VESTAVIA HILLS
LIBRARY IN THE FOREST
1221 MONTGOMERY HWY.
VESTAVIA HILLS, AL 35216
205-978-0155